On the Pitch

STARS OF MEN'S SOCCER

MEGAN COOLEY PETERSON

WORLD BOOK

BOLT

This World Book edition of *Stars of Men's Soccer* is published by agreement between Black Rabbit Books and World Book, Inc.
© 2018 Black Rabbit Books,
2140 Howard Dr. West,
North Mankato, MN 56003 U.S.A.
World Book, Inc.,
180 North LaSalle St., Suite 900,
Chicago, IL 60601 U.S.A.

All rights reserved. No part of this book may be reproduced in any form without written permission from the publisher.

Marysa Storm, editor; Michael Sellner, designer; Omay Ayres, photo researcher

Library of Congress Control Number: 2016049976

ISBN: 978-0-7166-9344-4

Printed in the United States at CG Book Printers, North Mankato, Minnesota, 56003. 3/17

Image Credits

Alamy: Action Plus Sports Images, 4–5, 15; A.F. ARCHIVE, 17 (right); ALBERT GEA / REUTERS, 9; Everett Collection Historical, 24; PA Images, 1, 25, Back Cover; Trinity Mirror / Mirrorpix, 6–7; AP Images: Ducklau/Schlagmann, 8; Getty Images: Carmen Flores / Stringer, 29; Miguel Tovar/LatinContent, Cover; Shutterstock: beltsazar, 21 (Beckham); EFKS, 20–21 (Stadium); katatonia82, 21 (Neuer); Krivosheev Vitaly, 3, 17 (left); makeitdouble, 28; Marcos Mesa Sam Wordley, 12–13, 19; Maxisport, 26; mooinblack, 20 (Hazard); Natursports, 20 (Messi); Oleh Dubyna, 21 (Ronaldo); Pal2iyawit, 22; Paolo Bona, 16; SSSCCC, 31; Vectomart, 6, 13, 32; USA Today Sports, Greg M. Cooper, 10; Winslow Townson, 20 (Neymar)
Every effort has been made to contact copyright holders for material reproduced in this book. Any omissions will be rectified in subsequent printings if notice is given to the publisher.

Contents

CHAPTER 1
Taking the Pitch......5

CHAPTER 2
The Stars............8

CHAPTER 3
Impressing Fans.....28

Other Resources...........30

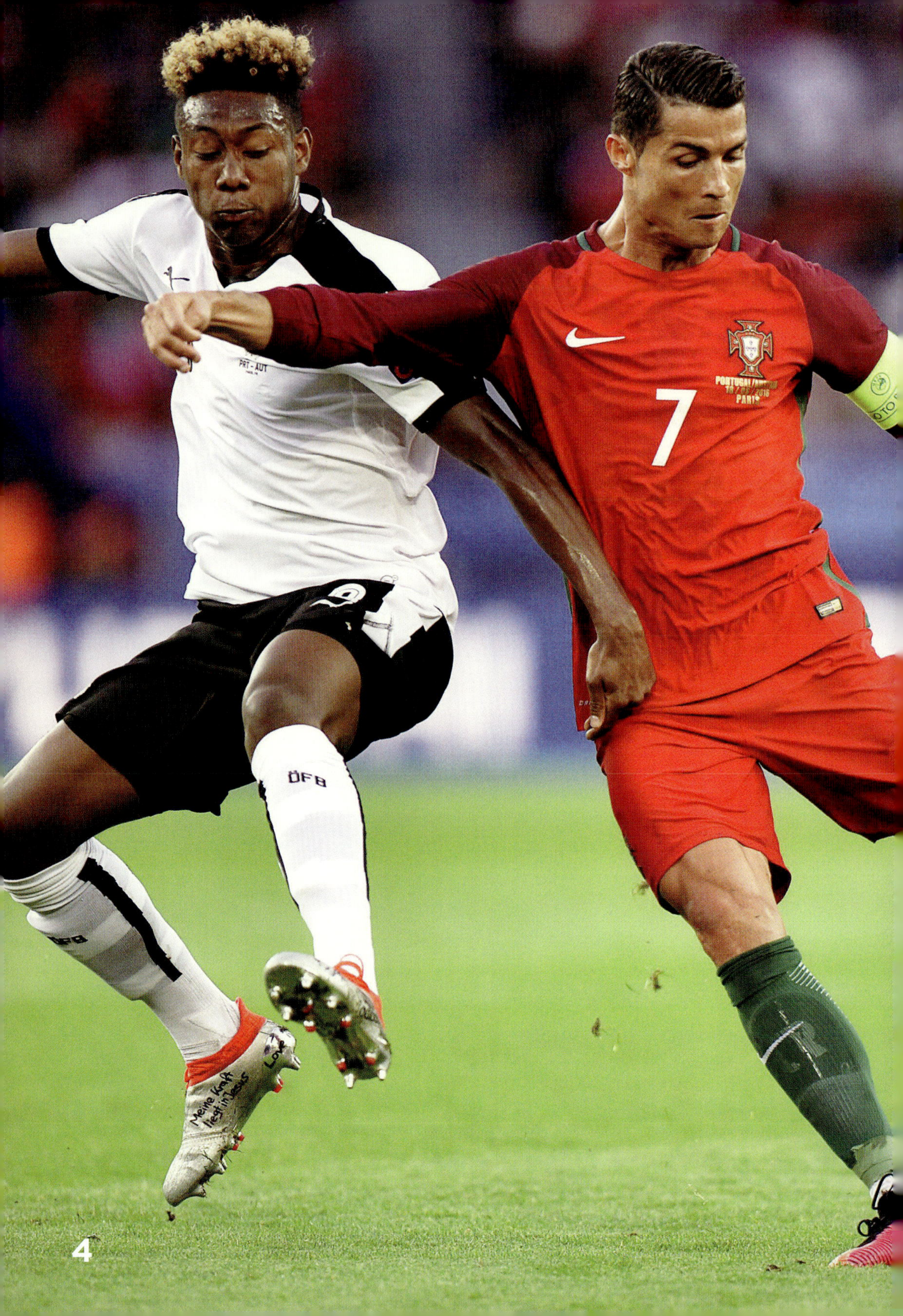
PRT - AUT
7
PORTUGAL
PARIS
ÖFB
Meine Kraft liegt in Jesus

CHAPTER 1

Taking the Pitch

A player dashes across the **pitch**. He races by a **defender**. He shoots the ball. It flies past the goalkeeper. Score!

Fans around the world follow men's soccer stars. Learn more about the players who wow crowds.

History of Men's Soccer

1863 — England's Football Association (FA) forms. It controls soccer in England.

1900 — First men's Olympic soccer game is held.

1904

International Federation of Association Football (FIFA) forms. FIFA controls world soccer.

Brazil wins its fifth World Cup. It holds the record for most World Cup wins.

● 2002

● 1958

● 2016

Pelé becomes the youngest player to score at the World Cup.

Real Madrid wins a record 11th Champions League title.

First World Cup tournament is held in Uruguay. Uruguay beats Argentina 4–2.

CHAPTER 2

The Stars

Lionel Messi

Lionel Messi has no trouble finding the net. He scored 91 goals in 2012. He broke Gerd Muller's record. Muller made 85 goals in 1972.

In 2015, Messi helped his team win the Champions League trophy.

As a kid, Messi was small for his age.

Doctors discovered he wasn't growing normally. He needed medicine to help him grow.

Number of Times Named FIFA World Player of the Year
as of 2016

Lionel Messi 5

Cristiano Ronaldo 4

Ronaldinho

Ronaldinho has slick footwork. It confuses defenders. While **dribbling**, he quickly flicks the ball left and right. He looks one way. Then he runs the other. This move is called the flip-flap.

Ronaldo	Zinedine Zidane	Ronaldinho
3	3	2

Dressed for Success

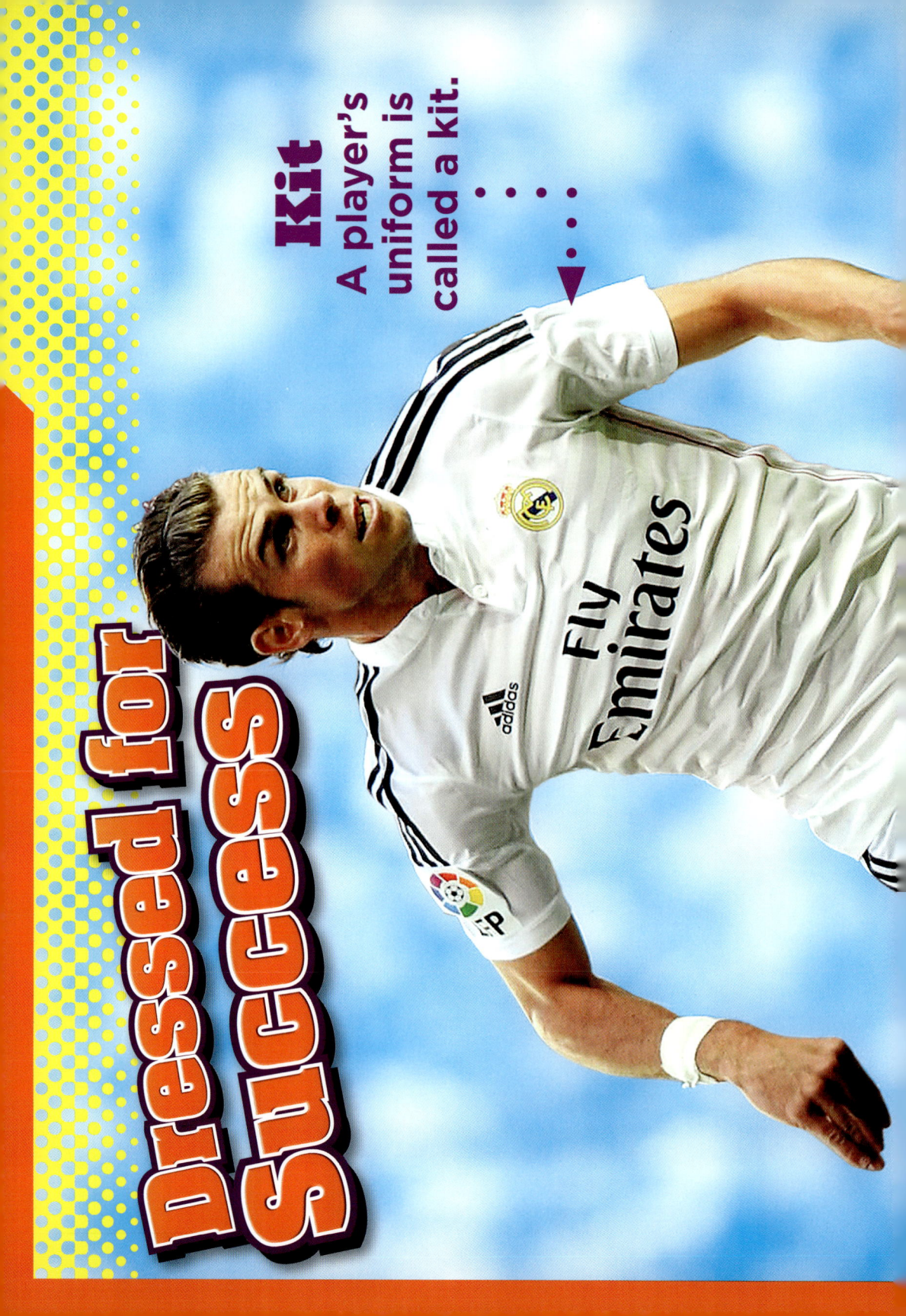

Kit
A player's uniform is called a kit.

Ball

WEIGHT
14 to 16 OUNCES
(397 to 454 grams)

CIRCUMFERENCE
27 to 28 INCHES
(69 to 71 centimeters)

Shin guards
Shin guards protect a player's legs.

Boots
Soccer shoes are called boots.

Manuel Neuer

Manuel Neuer is a German goalkeeper. Most goalkeepers stay within the white lines by the goal. But Neuer leaves the penalty area to make plays. He kicks and hurls the ball down the field. His moves impress many fans. Some fans say he is the greatest goalkeeper.

Neuer won the 2014 World Cup Golden Glove. It is awarded to the best goalkeeper.

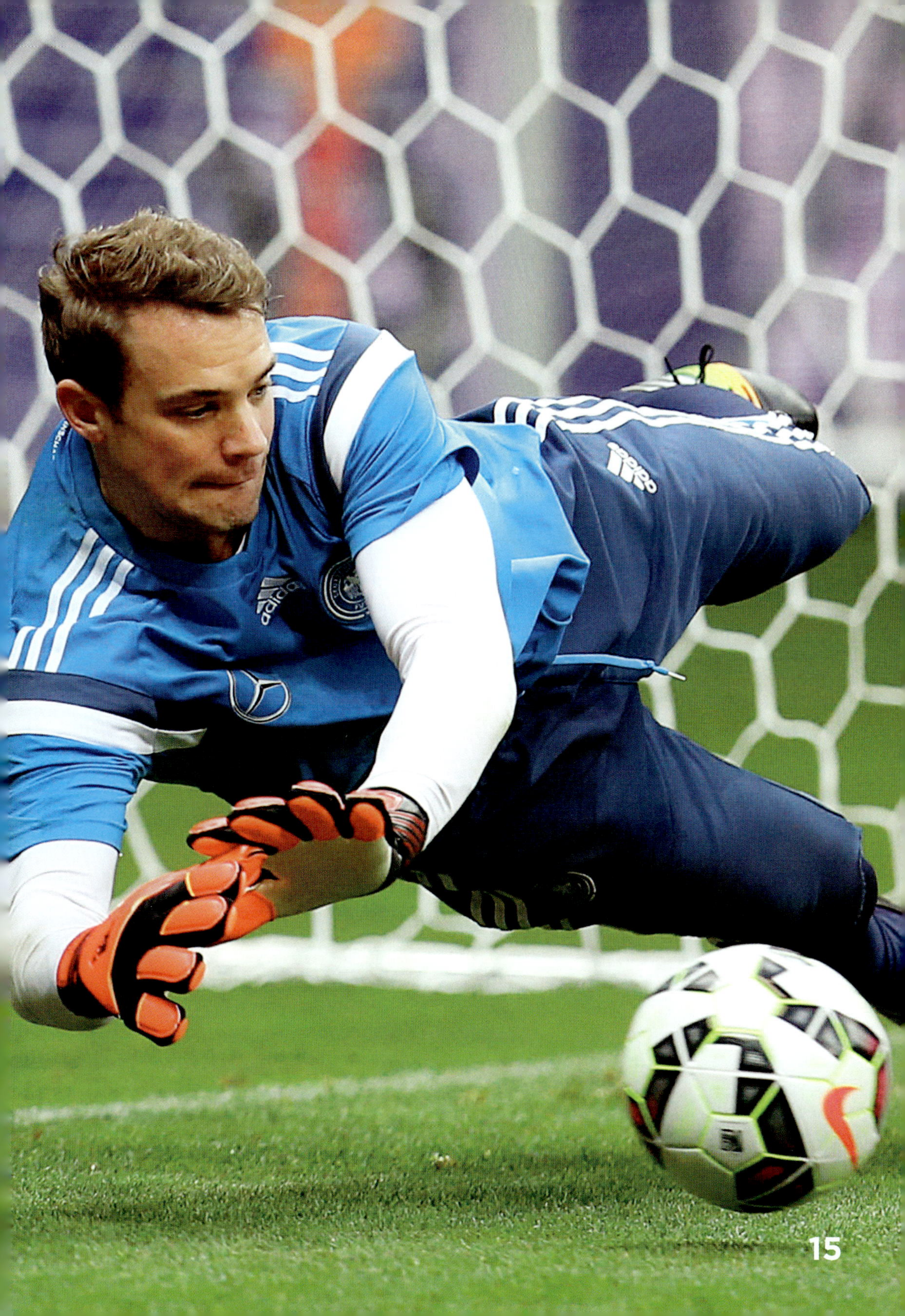
adidas
adidas

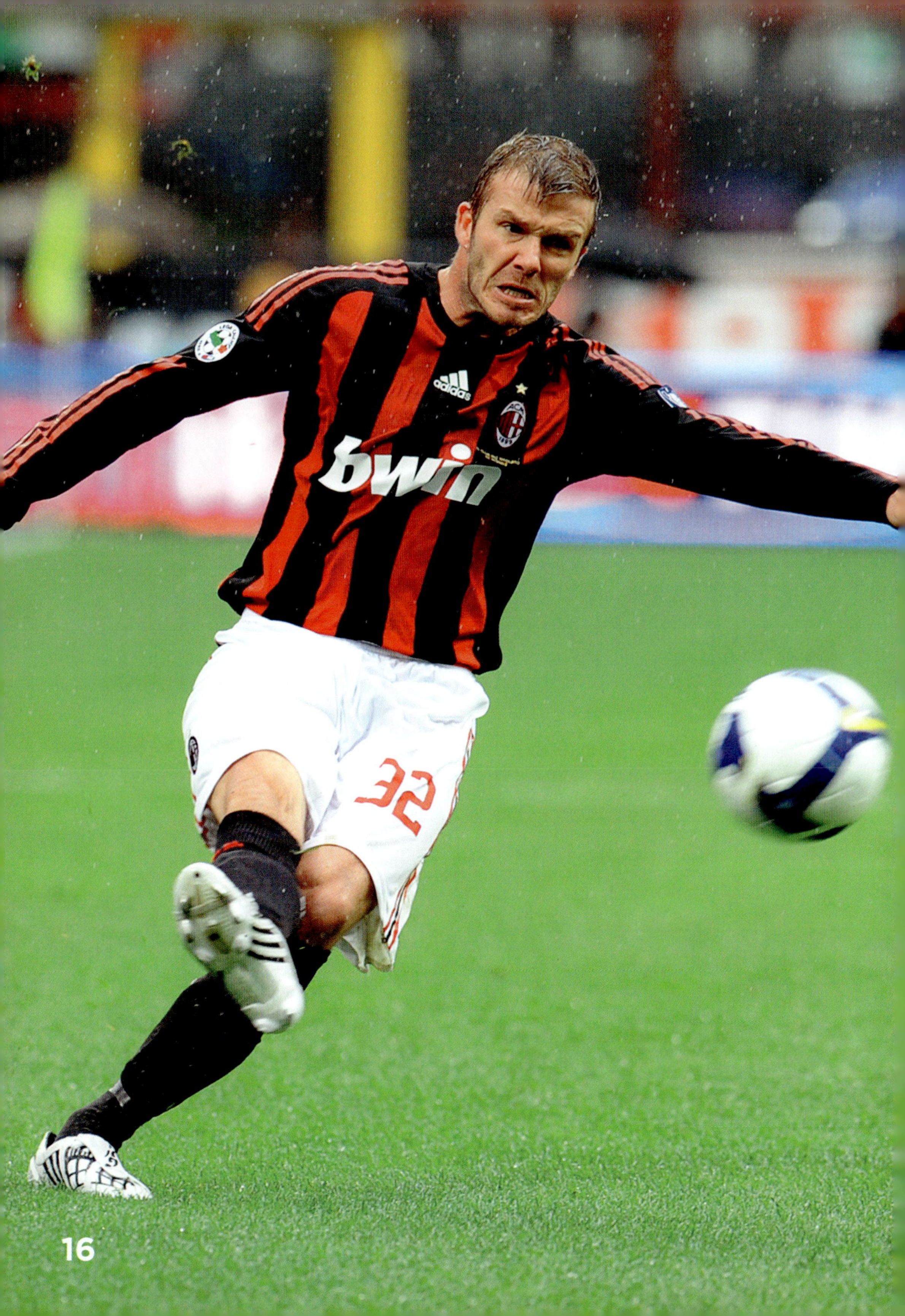
adidas
bwin
32

David Beckham

What's more famous than David Beckham? His right foot! Beckham was a master at **free kicks**. He could bend the ball around defenders.

The movie *Bend It Like Beckham* was named for his free kicks.

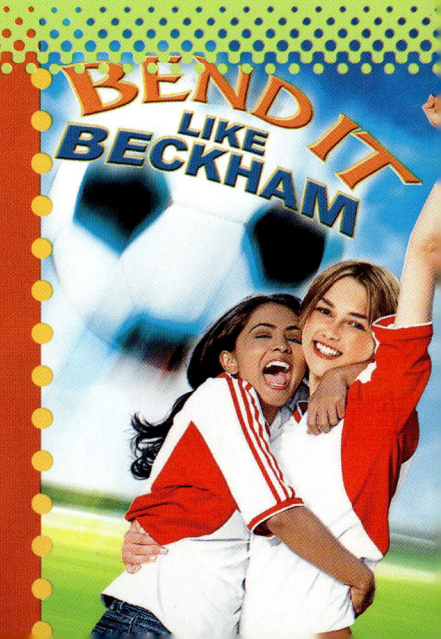

Cristiano Ronaldo

Cristiano Ronaldo is a **forward**. He has a fast style. His speed makes him tough to beat. He played for Manchester United. He led them to three league championships. They won the Champions League trophy in 2008. He also won the Champions League with Real Madrid twice.

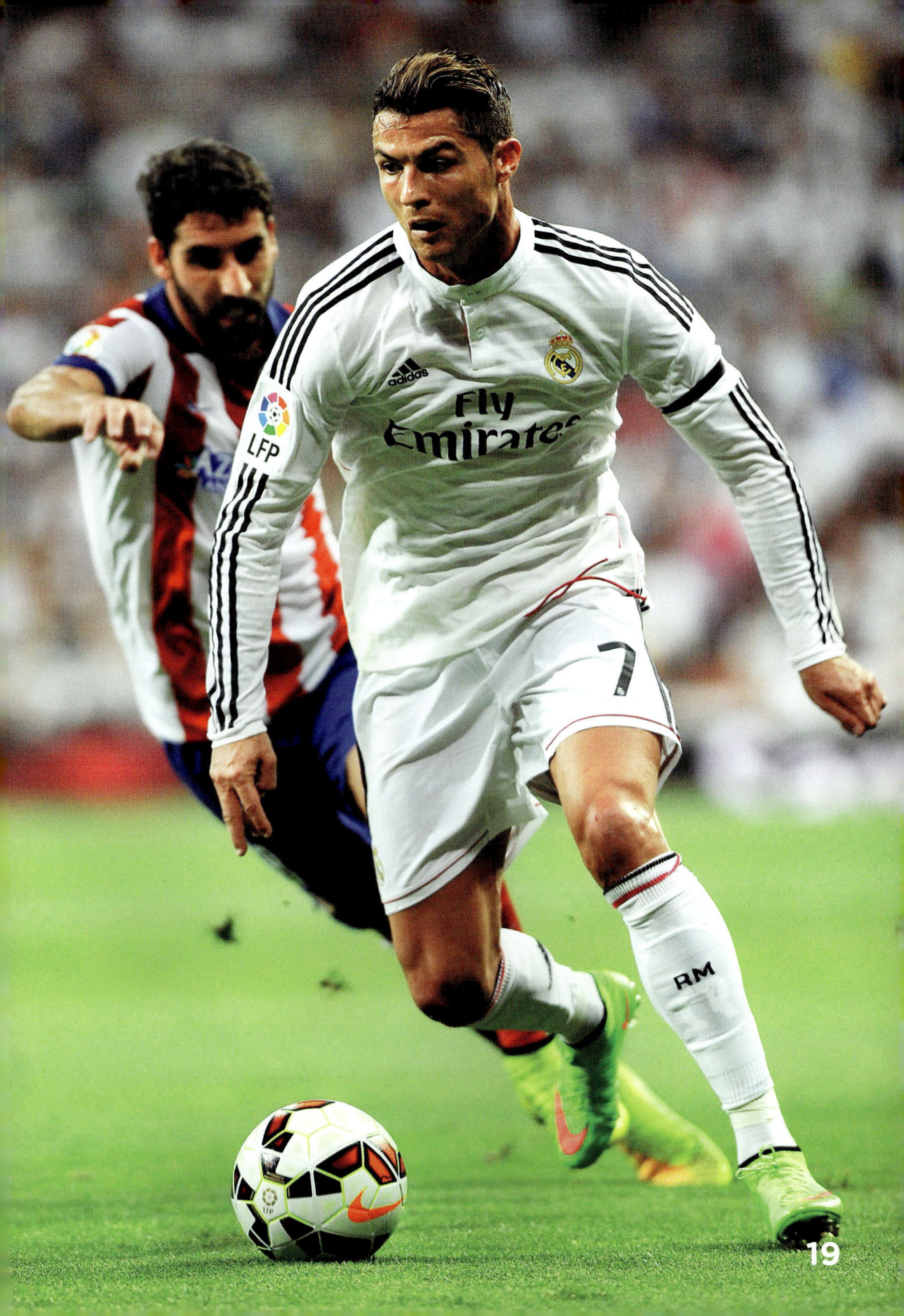
adidas
Fly
Emirates
LFP
7
RM

SIZING UP THE COMPETITION

HEIGHT (inches)

Player	Weight	Height
Lionel Messi	159 pounds (72 kilograms)	67" (170 cm)
Pelé	160 pounds (73 kg)	68" (173 cm)
Eden Hazard	163 pounds (74 kg)	68" (173 cm)
Neymar	150 pounds (68 kg)	69" (175 cm)

WEIGHT (pounds)

Player	Height	Weight
Ronaldinho	71" (180 cm)	176 pounds (80 kg)
David Beckham	72" (183 cm)	170 pounds (77 kg)
Gareth Bale	72" (183 cm)	163 pounds (74 kg)
Cristiano Ronaldo	73" (185 cm)	176 pounds (80 kg)
Manuel Neuer	76" (193 cm)	203 pounds (92 kg)

EYES
Players watch the field for the ball and other players.

LEGS
Players need strong leg muscles to run and kick.

ABDOMINALS
Strong abs help players balance while running.

ANKLES
Strong ankles allow players to change direction often.

Eden Hazard

Eden Hazard is a **midfielder**. He blazes past defenders. He has no problem scoring. He helps his teammates score too. Hazard was named 2015 PFA Player of the Year. PFA stands for Professional Footballers' Association.

STAYING HEALTHY

Top soccer players must stay in good shape.

Pelé

Some say Pelé changed soccer. He had especially quick footwork. No one had seen it before. He flew past defenders. He led Brazil to three World Cup wins. No other player has won that many Cups.

In 2002, a fan bought a Pelé jersey for more than $200,000.

Neymar

Some call Neymar the new Pelé. He plays for Barcelona. He was the team's second-highest scorer during the 2014–2015 season. Only teammate Messi scored more goals.

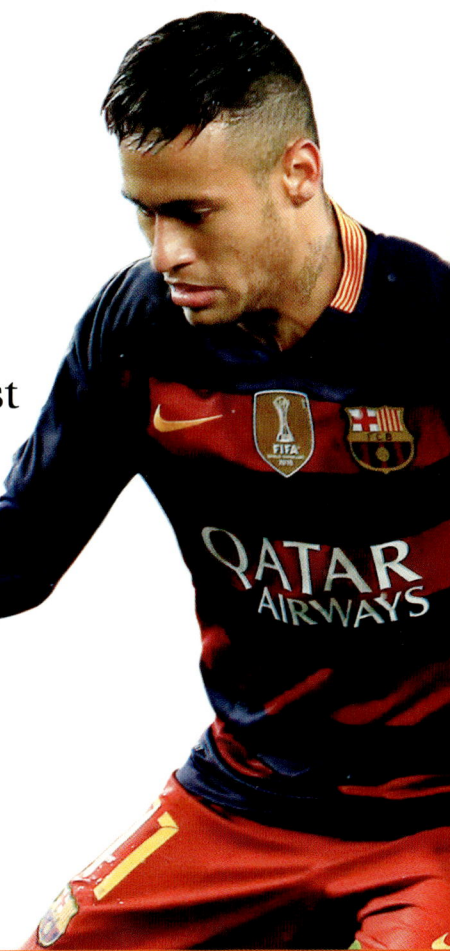

Pelé VS. Neymar

as of 2016

Pelé		Neymar
forward	position	forward
10	jersey number	10
dribbling, passing, and speed	known for	dribbling and passing
12	World Cup goals	4

Cristiano Ronaldo traded from Manchester United to Real Madrid for about $111 million

Gareth Bale traded from Tottenham to Real Madrid for about $106.6 million

Luis Suarez traded from Liverpool to Barcelona for about $99.5 million

dollars $0 $20,000,000 $40,000,000

Gareth Bale

Gareth Bale is a midfielder. He plays for Real Madrid. He dominated during the 2013–2014 season. He scored more than 20 goals. Bale helped his team win the Champions League.

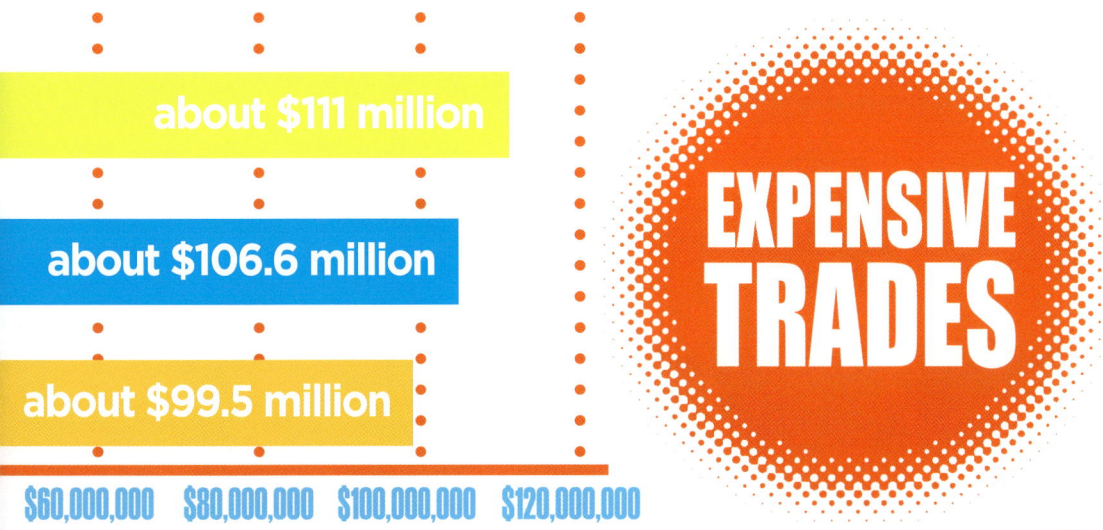

about $111 million

about $106.6 million

about $99.5 million

$60,000,000 $80,000,000 $100,000,000 $120,000,000

EXPENSIVE TRADES

CHAPTER 3

Impressing Fans

The stars of men's soccer attract fans around the world. Their kicks and footwork make games fun. They keep everyone wanting more.

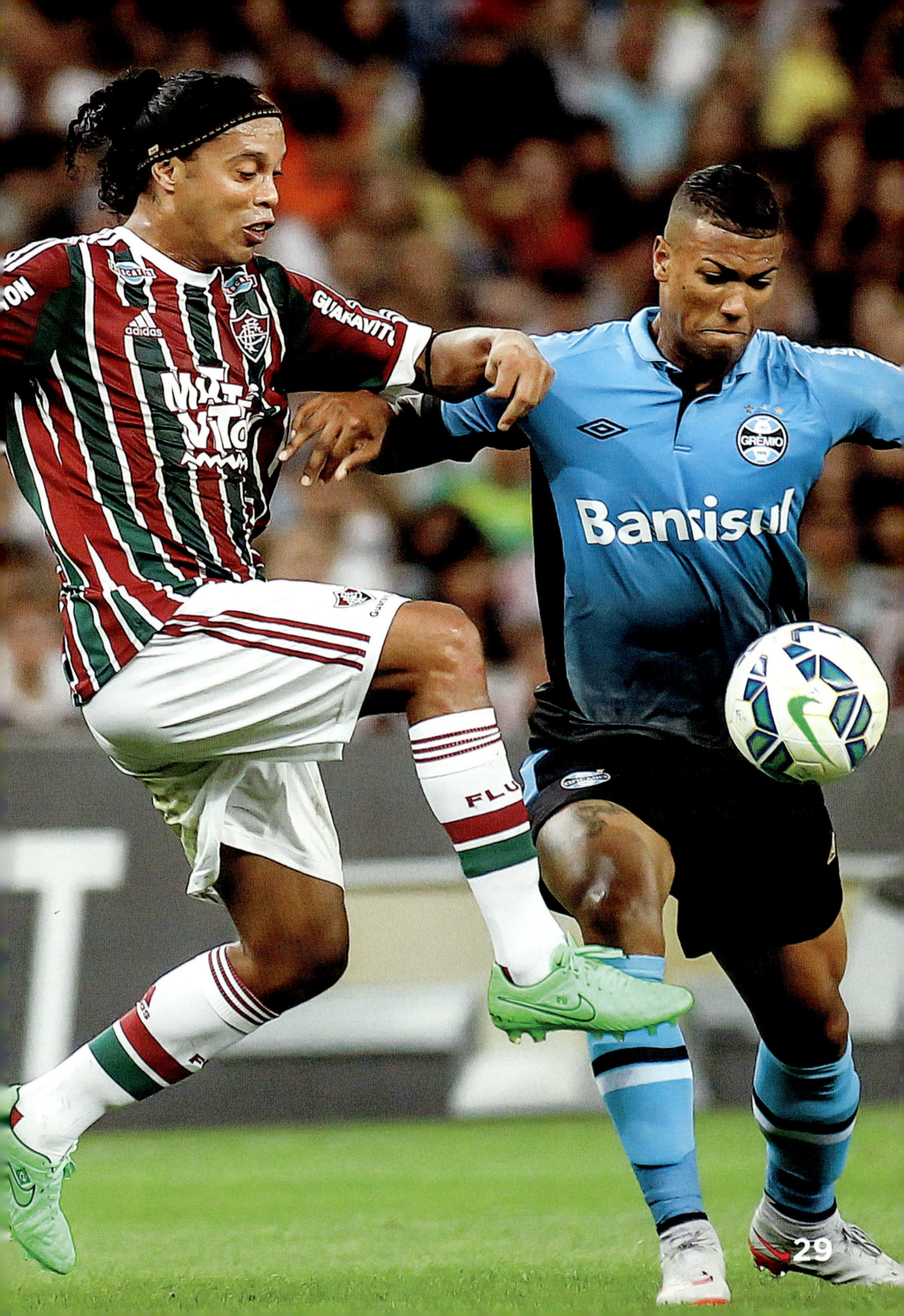
adidas
Banrisul
GRÊMIO
FLU

GLOSSARY

Champions League (CHAM-pee-uhnz LEEG)—a club contest for European soccer teams; the winner gets the Champions League trophy.

defender (de-FEN-dur)—a player who works to stop the other team from scoring

dribble (DRI-buhl)—to move the ball along by kicking it with the feet

forward (FOR-wurd)—a soccer player whose main job is to move the ball toward the opponent's goal and try to score

free kick (FREE KIK)—a kick taken after a penalty; a free kick is taken from the spot of a foul.

midfielder (MID-feel-dur)—a soccer player who plays in the middle of the field; midfielders feed the ball to the forwards and also score goals.

pitch (PICH)—a soccer field

tournament (TUR-nuh-muhnt)—a series of matches between several teams, ending in one winner

World Cup (WURLD CUP)—a soccer competition held every four years; teams from around the world compete against each other.

LEARN MORE

BOOKS
Kortemeier, Todd. *Superstars of World Soccer.* Pro Sports Superstars. Mankato, MN: Amicus High Interest, 2017.

Morreale, Marie. *Lionel Messi.* Real Bios. New York: Children's Press, 2016.

Murray, Laura K. *Cristiano Ronaldo.* The Big Time. Mankato, MN: Creative Education, 2016.

WEBSITES
Pelé
www.biography.com/people/pelé-39221

Soccer (Football)
www.ducksters.com/sports/soccer.php

U.S. Men's National Soccer Team
www.ussoccer.com/mens-national-team

INDEX

B

Bale, Gareth, 21, 26–27

Beckham, David, 17, 21

H

Hazard, Eden, 20, 23

history, 6–7

M

Messi, Lionel, 8, 9, 10, 20, 25

N

Neuer, Manuel, 14, 21

Neymar, 20, 25

P

Pelé, 7, 20, 24, 25

R

Ronaldinho, 11, 21

Ronaldo, Cristiano, 10, 18, 21, 26–27